Grieving Victoriously

Don't Allow the Grip of Grief
To Steal Your Hope and Calling

———— • ————

By Cindy Hutchison

Grieving Victoriously: Don't Allow the Grip of Grief to Steal Your Hope and Calling

By Cindy Hutchison

Copyright © 2021

ISBN: 978-0-578-97257-2

E-book ISBN: 978-0-578-97261-9

Cover Art by Olivia Avischious

Cover Design by Olivia Avischious - kilnliterary.com

Editing and Interior Design by Sarah Miles - kilnliterary.com

Proofreading by Jessica Bussell

Printed in the United States of America.

Dedication

To my husband, Jon. After all these years together, you are still the one I can't wait to come home to. I'm so grateful for you, and that our life together has been built on the Lord Jesus. We have been through much; yet, in our darkest time, you have always remained stable, loving, kind, and faithful to the Lord and our family. You are the dad our boy wanted to grow up to be. Thank you for all you are to me, our girls, and their families. I love you with all my heart.

To my beautiful girls, Melody Joy and Alexandra Leigh. You are my treasures on earth. You have kept your sweet, loving, and kind spirits, and remained faithful to the Lord in the good times and the very hard times, even when you watched your brother go through so much. Thank you for loving and respecting your daddy and me, even when we didn't know how rocky the road was going to get. You are both lovely and gracious young women, and this momma could not be more grateful or proud. I love you so.

To my son, Jon. I miss you more than words can say. You are my treasure in Heaven. I am so proud and grateful that I could be your mom, even if it was just for twenty-four short years. Thank you for teaching us what it was to be uncompromising in your walk with the Lord, to be loving to people who weren't always lovely by the world's standards, and giving your all when you could have given up. And—thank you for that crazy sense of humor that kept us in stitches. I love you so, and can't wait until we're all together again.

And to my Lord Jesus whom I love with everything within me—where would I be without You? You have been my constant throughout my life and have walked with me all my years. You truly are my Friend, Helper, Supply, Fortress, Comforter, Healer, Deliverer—every name that Scripture uses to describe You. Thank you for loving us, dying for us, giving us new life and a hope that cannot be destroyed. Because of all You did for us, one day, we will all be together again, worshiping around Your throne. Oh, what a day that will be!!

Yours O Lord is the greatness, the power,
the glory, the victory, and the majesty.
Everything in the heavens and on earth is
Yours, O Lord, and this is Your kingdom. We
adore You as the one who is over all things.

1 Chronicles 29:11 (New Living Translation)

Contents

Foreword

Thank you for allowing me to share these words with you. I have seen so many struggle with loss, and my heart goes out to every person of every age when I see how grief robs, tears down, and takes away hopes, dreams, and callings. I feel that God has called me, with the help of the Holy Spirit, to write this book to help you take back your life that has been ravaged by loss. I'm hopeful it will be a catalyst to help you heal what loss has affected in your heart and walk with God. While my experience is specifically with the loss of a child, I know that the loss of anything meaningful or precious can cause crippling grief. I trust that it will minister to anyone who has encountered devastation, even if it differs from my circumstances.

First, a word on what this book is. This book is foremost a way for you to know that you're not alone in what you're going through. This "club" is one that no one wants to belong to, and bigger than I ever imagined. I pray that it is also encouragement for you to know that there is still life to live and for you to be able to live it again, encouragement to know you can give yourself back to God and trust Him again, and encouragement to know that God has plans for you. You weren't created to stay under the covers and live the rest of your life in devastation. Lastly, I hope this book can be a way to understand that it really isn't all about you (I know this sounds harsh, but I hope you understand what I mean when I expound on this later). Grief has a way of making us selfish and taking away our life with the rest of our family and friends, along with our relationship with God. My hope is that this will help you recognize when grief may be taking control of your life and actions.

It might also help to define what this book is not. It is not a "self-help" book to help you move through the grieving process faster. It's called a Grieving Process for a reason. One of the definitions of "process" is that it's a series of actions or steps taken to achieve a particular end. By its very definition, you have to continue to move forward, but nowhere does it say it is a sprint. I have discovered that grieving is as unique for each person as snowflakes—it doesn't look the same for any two people, nor is the timeline the same for any two people.

If you are a well-meaning friend or relative who feels like this may help a family member "snap out of it," please remember, this will never go away. It is always present in this person's life, albeit in different stages. If they are less than six months into the grieving process, or even just a year, please be patient, they may not be ready for this book yet.

In the years since losing those that I love so much, I have realized that the process of grieving doesn't ever stop. That person or those persons don't quit existing in your memories, and the vacant places at your table don't suddenly become filled. Those you have lost are a part of your life that will continually be missed. They will forever be in your heart and you will always love and grieve for them. There will be times when your heart will nearly burst from missing them, and other times you feel like you're doing pretty well, then feel guilty for feeling that way. That is part of the grieving process, and it is never-ending. My opinion is that anyone who would try to tell you differently is incorrect.

Please know, I am not a PhD., a professional counselor, or even a college graduate. I am just a mom who has lost a child, and a daughter who has lost both of her parents. I also have spoken with friends who have gone through great losses different than mine. This information is based on my experiences and is not intended to treat or cure anyone. I do hope, however, that it can be an encouragement to those of you struggling since losing your loved one.

I have written this book with a "conversational approach," as if we were having coffee, and you were sharing your heart with me, and I with you. It is written from my experiences and from speaking with others to encourage and give you hope in this process. I used to think that only the loss through death was the source of grief; but, in my years, I have realized there are many sources of loss—the loss of a loved one, loss of innocence, loss of a marriage, loss of a business or finances, and many more. The experience of loss (for me the loss of family members, namely my child) is probably the deepest wilderness experience you will ever have. As I am editing this, I know of two mothers who buried their babies this week, due to being born much too early. My heart breaks for those mommas whose hopes and dreams for these little ones will never be realized on this earth. Some of you have lost your child by their own hand, and have left you not only grieving, but with many unanswered questions. My heart goes out to you with much compassion.

Since losing my son, I've come to realize, that it doesn't really matter when you lost your child, whether they were still in your womb, or you are advanced in age and your child was grown and getting older, themself. This loss is something that is devastating, and there will never be one time that is better than another. Many of you have experienced different losses than what I have experienced. I have two friends who lost their husbands at a young age, leaving each of them with three young children to raise. Over the years I've seen friends and acquaintances suffer different losses than these. While the loss can be different, the end result is the same—devastating grief. While I will be speaking mainly to the loss that I've experienced, if you are reading this and have experienced a loss different than mine, I trust that what I have written will minister to you also.

The core message of my experience is as follows: We have to have God as our focus and hope. Only He can truly put the pieces back together with the counsel and the comfort of the Holy Spirit. As I understand, focusing our attention on our Heavenly Father can be a hard thing after the loss of our loved ones. But, I also know that without Him, we can do nothing.

I believe the Lord laid it on my heart to put this book in the format you see before you to help you through this process. Some of you will read slowly and spend much time journaling in between chapters. You will see that there are questions and journaling pages at the end of each chapter. These are for you to write down your thoughts, prayers, even your cries or your heartache. If you are frustrated at God, or upset about a situation that brought all the pain back again, write it down. You may go back and read after a time and see how much you have grown. Or, you may be like me, and not yet be able to look at what you wrote because the pain is just too much. Regardless, writing those things down can help give an outlet to some of your heartache. Some of you may need to write a lot, and some of you may write a little, or even nothing. Some of you may take a long time between chapters, and others of you may move quickly, depending on where you are in your process. Some of you may want to do this as a study together with friends or in a group so you can share your heart, your tears, and your hurts to support each other while you go through it. Some of you may want to read this on your own to keep things between you and God. You may want to move straight through the book, or you may want to skip chapters because they speak to something in your heart that you're just not ready to take on yet. You can always come back to them later.

Some of these chapters will apply to you almost immediately; and, for others, it will be some time before it applies. Remember, there is much liberty in this book - how to read it, when to read it, and when to apply it to your life. There may be a chapter that you need to skip for a while, and go to another chapter. Remember, the important thing is that you don't stay in the same place forever, in this book, as well as on your life journey.

This book is yours to use for your process— no one else's. It is to help encourage you in living in this "new normal," and do what you are called to do while moving forward. My hope is that this book will allow you to live life to its fullest for the part of the process you're in. That even in grief, you will be able to continue walking, not wake up every day and only exist with the covers over your head (I mean that both figuratively and literally). My prayer is that you will *Press In* to God. In this context, the definition of "Pressing In" is to spend concerted time in God's word and in prayer. This is a phrase you will see throughout the book. I truly believe that without God's grace and mercy, you can never be filled with power to move ahead in your calling. I pray that you will seek Him, and that even though your "why" questions may not be answered on this earth, that as time moves on you will realize you have a hope and a calling, and you can continue to move forward as you Press In to the One who loves you more than any other, who knows you, and sees your heartache and your tears.

*You've kept track of my every toss
and turn through the sleepless nights.
Each tear written in Your ledger, each
ache written in Your book.*

Psalm 56:8 (The Message)

Introduction

By Cheryl Wright
Author of *His Warrior Princess: A Girlfriend's Guide to Being Lit From Within*

C.S. Lewis once said: "Grief is like a long valley, a winding valley where any bend may reveal a totally new landscape." Grief and loss inevitably touch us in different ways throughout the journey of life. We were unfortunately never promised a life free of trials and loss, but we were promised His Presence would lead us through every valley of weeping and every season of sorrow. Sometimes, it is a lonely road of loss we walk and it is reassuring to have someone there beside us.

You are probably holding this book in your hands because death and loss has touched you in some aspect. The author of this book is someone who has walked a similar path and as you read her story of grief and dealing with the loss of her beloved son, she will help you navigate the bends in the road. Cindy's honest and transparent recounting of her story helps the reader understand they are not alone on the journey of grief. She is someone who has navigated the winding valley of loss which Lewis alluded to and she can give you some travel tips and rest station locations along the way.

In Deuteronomy 31:6 the Lord encourages us He walks the road with us and will never leave us. As you read this book, may you sense the Lord's Presence and may Cindy's words be like a glass of refreshing water to a travel-weary soul.

Chapter 1

Freedom from the Grip of Grief

After the loss of my son, the only thing that my heart desired was to be free from the onslaught of grief. I was desperate for everything to be back to normal, but that is something that I knew I could never have. The grip of grief was tight like a vice on my every thought. How can you find freedom from the grip of grief when your heart has been ripped apart?

———— • ————

Dear brothers and sisters, when troubles of any kind come your way, consider it an opportunity for great joy. For you know that when your faith is tested, your endurance has a chance to grow. So let it grow for when your endurance is fully developed, you will be perfect and complete, needing nothing.

James 1:2-4 *(The Passion Translation)*

———— • ————

How can we "consider it an opportunity for great joy" when we have experienced such devastation that wants to tear us apart? Some of you may be thinking, "You've got to be kidding me!!! I have lost my child, my husband, my parents, my sibling, my health, my home, my marriage, my business, my job, my _____!! There is no way I will ever consider this joy!!" I totally understand. I felt the same way. But, I don't believe that Scripture is telling us that the situation that happened is supposed to bring joy to our hearts. Our Heavenly Father knows us better than that. However, the growth and healing that can come from what has happened in our lives can eventually bring us joy.

Now, before you decide to close this book because you can't relate to this verse, and think, "This lady has got it all together. I'm not in that place and I can't do that," let me share a little of my story with you. In 2006, we were enjoying our family. Our oldest daughter had graduated from a wonderful Christian University, and we were so grateful to have her back with us. She was working and living at home temporarily while she waited for her dream job to become available. Our twenty-two-year-old son had just finished a three-year internship program where he had literally gone to the uttermost parts of the earth to preach the gospel and assist other pastors in doing so, and was ready to take the world by storm. He was looking at becoming a youth pastor or a missions pastor. Our younger daughter was seventeen, blooming into womanhood, growing in the Lord, enjoying great friendships (which she still enjoys to this day), working hard in school, and attending church activities.

We were enjoying watching our kids grow and seeing what doors God was opening for each of them. A few weeks after our son graduated from his internship program, he started having horrible headaches and dizziness. It was shortly after that, that we discovered he had a brain tumor. We believed God had a strong call on his life and completely believed that He was going to heal him. After all, why would God *not* want to heal a young man so dedicated to Him who wanted to go to the uttermost parts of the earth for His kingdom? We prayed fervently (at one time we believe there were around 50,000 people around the world petitioning God for His healing) and used all the medical expertise we had at our disposal. We fought for nearly two and a half years—with two brain surgeries, chemo, radiation, and even a stem cell transplant—but to no avail. We lost him on the twelfth of October, 2008. He was an amazing young man—handsome, funny, compassionate, and uncompromising in his faith.

I guess you could say that I am a mom who loves her children fiercely. All of my children would attest to that, and to be completely helpless to do anything for this wonderful boy of mine was completely devastating to me. I thought God didn't love me anymore to allow such a thing, or that I must have done something horribly wrong for this to happen to our family. In my striving to figure out what God was thinking, I have asked and made these comments to Him many times over: "So, you didn't need someone who wanted to go to the uttermost parts of the earth and share the gospel?" "I thought my Heavenly Father wanted to give good gifts to His children! This was not a good gift!" Believe it or not, I still go there at times. Of course, my biggest question that I still ask even today is, "Why?" I sometimes wonder if God gets tired of hearing that question, because I still can't wrap my head around something that, in my finite mind, makes no sense. Even after all these years, I still break down. I was in a store a while back, and when it hit me that while most people were looking for flowers for their Christmas décor, I was looking for flowers to put at my boy's grave for Christmas, I lost it. Even now after all these years that we have been putting flowers at his grave, that one day, the injustice of it all and the loss hit me all over again.

My mother-in-law was taken from us suddenly, just a couple of years before my son became ill. She was much too young—and was still very vital—as well as a very gracious, wise, and kind lady. When she left us, it was a complete shock to our entire family, and left us wondering, "Why?" Her passing left a huge hole in the hearts of our family that has never been filled, and I miss her dearly.

On the other hand, my parents were quite elderly when they passed away. They both passed in 2011, eight months apart, to the day. I always thought that if my parents were elderly that it wouldn't affect me in the same way as if I lost them at a different time. I was amazed at how it threw me for a loop for nearly a year after they left here for Heaven. This was my mommy and my daddy who loved me, cared for me, raised me to know and love Jesus, loved my husband like he was their own, and were Grandad and Grandmom to my children, whom they loved so much. They were funny, loving, kind, and served God with all that they had. My mom struggled with dementia for several years and my dad struggled with side effects from all the medications he was on. They became shadows of their former selves, and no longer were the mom and dad that gave wisdom, counsel, and prayed fervently for my family and my siblings' families. Even when they were still living, our visits were no longer about telling stories, laughter over a joke or pun, or giving counsel. Though they served God fervently, they were empty shells of who they used to be before they left this earth. I miss them and who they used to be more than I could have imagined. Again, I wonder *why* God would allow this to happen to such wonderful people.

My story most likely doesn't look like any of your stories. We all have different devastating situations, different relationships with those we lost, and different timelines. The people we lost were anywhere in age from still being in the womb to the elderly. At the same time, we all have one thing in common. We have lost those whom we loved, and who had great influence on our lives, and it is devastating. For others, you have lost your livelihood, physical abilities, homes, businesses, friendships, etc. We've all had our lives devastated by situations outside our control, and for some, it has left us without the ability to get out of bed, put one foot in front of the other, or even step outside our front door.

Please remember that I understand this process. I have experienced many of the different stages of grief. As I mentioned before, one of the definitions of process is a series of actions or steps taken to achieve a particular end. By its very definition, you have to continue to move. I have found that if you don't continue to move and live, your body, mind, and spirit will atrophy and die— figuratively, and, in some cases, literally.

How can we find freedom from the grip of grief when our heart has been ripped apart? How do we "consider it an opportunity for great joy" when we have such devastation that wants to rob us of all that we have believed?

Press in to your Heavenly Father. James 4:8 says, "Move your heart closer and closer to God, and He will come even closer to you" (The Passion Translation). You may feel like He has completely let you down, and He's not worth trusting. You may feel like His promises are not true, He's not really your friend, and that He doesn't care. When we lost our son, we were completely devastated, but our daughters were also devastated, as they truly loved their brother. The one thing I encouraged them to do was to "press in." They did, and when they could have turned away, they chose to continue to love and serve Jesus.

As for myself, I felt like I was at a crossroad, and I could either choose to continue to follow God, or to turn away from everything I had known since I was young. It was a very real crossroad for me. I had served God for nearly my entire life. I thought that should have meant something to Him and He should have saved my son to prove it. I struggled with this conflict for a long time. In the end, I knew that there was no one else or anything else worth serving, and that no matter what happened, I truly loved my Heavenly Father. But it also meant pressing into Him when I wasn't feeling it.

Does that mean that we all went on our merry way and never struggled with anything again? NO!! We couldn't be at any of the places where our son had been so active. Church became nearly impossible for us to attend. We would see where he used to worship, and the friends he would hang out with who were still getting to enjoy their lives, their families, and fulfill their callings. This place that used to be a safe harbor became a place of great hurt to our souls. We would try to go, and would end up leaving a short time later, because the memories and hurt just went too deep. Home became my safe haven. I would go to work, and would come straight home. It was the only place I felt I could truly be myself. I remember the pain would be so great, I would get home, run to our closet, and sob from something I had seen that would remind me of my son. I look back now and realize that I went through an angry time in my process. I didn't see it when I was in the middle of it, but people would comment at work that they didn't want to come and talk to me about a work situation because I was not kind in my answers. Now that I look back, I see that I was angry—angry at God, angry at people who had issues that were not as important as mine were (at least in my mind), and angry at the trite things they needed help with, when I was going through this great devastation. We all had things that we had to work through, and, ultimately, we needed to Press In to the Lord to be healed.

When many of us go through trials and tribulations, we are referred to the book of Job. It tells us that Job was very wealthy, had many children, and was the richest man in all the land, but due to the testing that God allowed in his life, he lost everything, including his children. It also says that due to his faithfulness to God, that after he had been tested, everything had been restored to him. For years, I just thought it was so great that God had been faithful and restored his fortune and his family, in giving him even more sons and daughters, until I lost my own child. While I imagine that Job was so grateful to the Lord for being faithful to him and restoring it all back, I couldn't help but think that he must have missed his other children greatly, missed the talks he had with his sons, or the sweet hugs he would get from his daughters. While his life was good and his "new normal" prosperous, I would think he still grieved for those precious ones he had lost. Scripture doesn't mention it, but I wonder how he dealt with those losses, while yet being so grateful to all God had restored.

Please remember that the enemy of your soul wants you to pull away and not give your time or attention to the Lord. He wants to stress that God must not love you to allow something so hurtful to happen, that He must not be a good Father, and He must not really care, so why should you care about Him? After your initial time of grieving, (which is not the same timeline for every person), it is time to Press In, even when you are still angry. It may only be for a few minutes to begin with, but allow the Lord back in and be like a balm to bring soothing to your spirit and your soul.

*Let this hope burst forth within you,
releasing a continual joy. Don't give up
in a time of trouble, but commune with
God at all times.*

Romans 12:12 (The Passion Translation)

Spend time with friends who know the
Father and know you. When you've gone through
such devastation, try not to hang out with friends
who want to justify your anger at God and what
has happened, as that can be the easier road to
take. Instead, spend time with friends who will
love you, encourage you, direct you to the Father,
and pray with you. When we've gone through
such a devastating time, it's easy to just want to be
alone with our thoughts. Don't become isolated.
That is where the enemy can trip you up.

Take every thought captive, "Casting down
arguments and every high thing that exalts itself
against the knowledge of God, bringing every
thought into captivity to the obedience of Christ"
2 Corinthians 10:5 (New King James Version).
The enemy wants you to feel sorry for yourself
and wallow in self-pity. It is easier to do that, but
that is not God's purpose or plan for you. You
are a walking testimony of this "new normal."
Wallowing in self-pity makes it harder to get out
of bed each morning. It keeps your eyes focused
on you. The longer you stay in that, you risk living
a life of bitterness, anger and complete anguish,
where nothing and no one will measure up to
what you once had. You run the risk of alienating

the people you love and the things you once enjoyed. Pressing into the One who knows you best and loves you most is the only way to keep from getting lost in that hopelessness and grip of grief.

1. How do you feel grief has gripped you?

2. Do you feel it has hindered your being able to move forward?

3. In what ways have you seen God help you through your grief?

4. What verse of Scripture has been particularly helpful in this stage of your walk?

_____

_____

_____

_____

_____

_____

_____

_____

_____

_____

_____

_____

_____

_____

Chapter 2

Freedom from Regrets and Guilt

The enemy of our souls wants us to live in the past. Regret and guilt are powerful tools to that end. The "accuser" wants us to live with a burden of regret and guilt that we can never escape from. Unfortunately, if we stay there, we can never be free to truly live again, and we will give opportunity for the enemy to get victory over our situation.

I lived there (and occasionally still do) for quite a while. I had thoughts that plagued my mind: *I should have taken more days off work to spend time with my boy. I should have done more research and questioned the doctors more. I should have pursued a cure for him myself. I should not have been in such denial of the statistics, and thought everything would be okay. I should not have had such faith that God would and had already healed him, then maybe I would have pursued my other regrets harder.* Then there were regrets I had about my girls—I wasn't spending enough time with them and giving them the attention they needed, especially my younger daughter in her senior year of high school. She came back from a missions trip from Germany the day before we found out about my son's illness, and we never got to really give her the time to tell us about it. Even writing this chapter brings back those feelings of regret. If we choose to dwell here we can get lost in a vortex of guilt and regret that we can never escape from and we can never truly be free.

For those of you who have these kinds of regrets, please know that I understand that for all of us who live with these regrets that these were our loved ones, and we did what we felt was the very best thing we could do with the resources we had at the time. Notice that each of my regrets wish to change what I did in the past. By the nature of regret, that is what it wants to do. However, there is nothing we can do to change the past. Even with that knowledge, regret will still haunt you. In the years since my son went to Heaven, I've found that regrets will always creep into my mind. I've made the choice that I will not camp there, and they will not control me. There are many times, even now, that those thoughts will come up and I will have to say, *Stop it Cindy!*, and call on the Lord for help. He always comes to my rescue, and I am able to put those thoughts behind me.

Don't allow those regrets to subtly work their way back in, as they will try. Once again, I will say this: Press In to your Heavenly Father. Cry out to Him. Bind and cast aside those regrets that are a tool of the enemy that want to continually creep back in and make it so you can't live your life. Allow the Holy Spirit to envelope your heart and bring comfort to your soul and spirit. That's why He's called the Comforter. He loves to do that. Hear this advice from Paul on what to fill our minds with instead of regret:

———•———

Summing it all up, friends, I'd say you'll do best by filling your minds and meditating on things true, noble, reputable, authentic, compelling, gracious—the best, not the worst; the beautiful, not the ugly; things to praise, not things to curse. Put into practice what you learned from me, what you heard and saw and realized. Do that and God, who makes everything work together, will work you into His most excellent harmonies.

Philippians 4:8-9 (The Message)

———•———

We are told to think on those things that are good and beautiful. May I suggest that when your mind takes you to the past—the domain so easily ruled by regret—that you think on the *good* times with your loved ones. As I say this, I'm reminded that I could not do this for quite a time after my son passed away. Those thoughts brought hurt and anger that he was no longer here, and brought those "why" questions into focus again. It was hard. It *is* hard. I am not saying that this will be something you can do immediately, but it is definitely something that you can revisit with time.

While we're on the subject, the saying "Time heals all wounds," I don't believe to be true at all. But, I do believe that time helps you learn to cope. It changes your perspective so that after a while, the memories that devastated you when you first experienced your loss, can put a smile on your face when you are able to go back and remember those happy times again without the burden of regret.

Once those regrets have surfaced less and less, and you feel that you have been able to start living again in this "new normal," I would encourage you to start thinking about your future. What did you feel was your calling or your dream before this devastation happened in your life? Has it been put on the backburner or completely discarded, due to what you have gone through? Or, has God "tweaked" it in some way? I never intended to write a book about my experience with grieving, but I always wanted to be able to speak to people—whether it would be in a Bible study, retreat, conference—whatever God allowed to be put in my path. God used my experience to "tweak" my heart's desire. My desire didn't change, but the subject matter did. If your calling or dream has been covered over by grief, when you are ready, I would encourage you to uncover it. Ask God where He wants to use you. Don't allow the enemy to steal your heart's desire from you. You are called to more than you ever knew. The enemy meant to use this time of grieving to make you forget it, or cause the flame to die out on the calling that God put in your heart, but God will take it, and will use it for good.

I've touched on guilt a little bit, but I have found all these emotions have a tendency to be connected with those things that hold us back from our hope and our calling. The enemy will use guilt to control our lives. Sometimes guilt can be a good emotion to hold us back from going the wrong way and pointing us in the way we need to go; but, it can also be an emotion that grabs us and holds on in such a way that we cannot get away from its grip, causing almost an emotional suffocation. After losing my son, I had a tendency to allow guilt to overtake me. It came in the form of regrets, or just the thought that I shouldn't enjoy what my son couldn't. I would look ahead to the years that I would have to spend without him and wonder how I could ever enjoy life again, when he was not here to enjoy it with us. Then, I would feel guilty, because, how could I love and support my girls and my husband and enjoy their joys and victories, without also feeling guilt over enjoying those joys and victories? Sometimes the thought of that was more than I could stand. It ended up being a vicious cycle. How could we be enjoying life's wonderful moments when he no longer could? How could I even think of that possibility?

Other people that I've spoken to have mentioned their guilt in this situation, too. We feel guilty if we enjoy anything because the loved one we lost can no longer enjoy those same things. It can leave you stuck in the grip of grief and guilt, not being able to move ahead, function, or even breathe. I've heard so many say that our loved ones would not want us to live this way. While your initial reaction to that cliche phrase may be to disregard it because it's a phrase that people use to try to snap you out of your grief, I actually do believe it's true for most of us. Through time and processing, I have learned to laugh and enjoy life again without guilt or remorse. You have loved ones who are still here on this earth who need you to laugh and celebrate with them, and the thought of never sharing in those things because of guilt can be heartbreaking—not only to them, but also to you.

I continually asked God "why" over and over. I am grateful that He is a God of love, grace, and patience, as I imagine I sounded a bit like a child who asks their parent the same question over and over. While the "why" question has not been answered, if I had actually stopped and listened to His still small voice, it probably wouldn't have taken so long for me to know that He actually was listening.

At some point, the light came on in my spirit. In my desire to understand all the "ifs," "ands," and "whys" with what happened to our son and the devastation to our family, the Lord spoke to me, and things took on a different light after that. If your loved one accepted Jesus as Lord and Savior in their lifetime, you can know with confidence that they are living life to the fullest with joy, laughter, music and love amplified beyond our comprehension. What they are enjoying in their lives makes our lives look like nothing but drudgery. They are not hampered by guilt, shame, hurt, frustration, money worries, health concerns—nothing. They are living in the presence of Almighty God. They are not in a grave or even in a container on your mantle. Yes, their earthy bodies are there, and a tangible source for us to honor and be close to, but their spirit—the very thing that made them who they were—is enjoying the fruits of Heaven. They do not deal with the "ifs," "ands," and "whys," or the guilt that follows with those questions. If given the choice, my guess is they would say they never would want to come back to this earth and face what we are facing daily. Since they are not dealing with those things, then why should we have to be overcome by them?

Now, what if your loved one didn't accept Jesus as Lord and Savior in their lifetime? That brings a completely different kind of grief and uncertainty into the process of dealing with their loss. I will come back to this point later in the book, but I will say that all we can do is trust that our God is Love, and He is actively pursuing His creation. None of our grief is overlooked by Him. Trusting Him reminds us that His plan is all-knowing *and* all-loving. If we get bogged down in the "ifs," "ands," and "whys," then that keeps us in the cycle of regret, guilt, and doubt, putting a barrier between us and our trust in God.

I also want to remind you that there is an enemy of your soul. The very one who brings this kind of guilt to your spirit, and wants nothing more than to see you wrapped up in this overwhelming fear and guilt. The enemy wants to kill, steal, and destroy your life and any possibility that you would fulfill the calling that God has for you. Don't allow him the satisfaction. When you are feeling this way, remember who is bringing this on you, and take authority over him. As a child of God, it is your right and your responsibility to do so. Don't allow the enemy to get a hold on you in this way.

Wherever you are in your grieving process, please remember that while this is part of the process, this is not where you are to camp. Scripture says, "Are you weary, carrying a heavy burden? Come to me. I will refresh your life, for I am your oasis" Matthew 11:28 (The Passion Translation). Press In and allow the Holy Spirit to bring refreshing and renewal to your spirit. You can keep moving, even if it seems like it is taking an eternity to do so. You can move out from under the cloud of guilt that grief wants to keep you under. Jesus will meet you at your point of need. You don't have to stay in the grip of sadness, never being able to smile or laugh again. You *can* experience times of victory and of joy even while going through this grieving process.

———— • ————

A thief has only one thing in mind—he wants to steal, slaughter, and destroy. But I have come to give you everything in abundance, more than you expect—life in its fullness until you overflow!

John 10:10 (The Passion Translation)

———— • ————

I have found that there will always be those times that sneak up on you when you least expect it, and try to steal the progress you've made. Sometimes it feels like you're taking three steps forward, and two, three, or even four steps back, and in my experience those are normal. But, as time goes on, I encourage you to take authority over those feelings and go deeper and deeper into the heart of God, even when you don't feel like it. Continue to Press In to Him. There, you can experience fullness of joy, great victories, and things you never thought possible (as I have, in writing this book). Give yourself permission to enjoy those victories and times of joy. Allow yourself new experiences, things that are fun and bring joy to your heart. Even though this process seems to be a never-ending part of life, allow it to truly be a process where you continually put one foot in front of the other, continue to move forward, and in that, give yourself freedom from regret and guilt, and the grace to live again.

1. Do you have regrets that you have had trouble moving past?

2. What has God helped you to overcome?

3. What verse of Scripture has been particularly helpful in this stage of your walk?

4. In what way has it ministered to you?

_____

_____

_____

_____

_____

_____

_____

_____

_____

_____

_____

_____

_____

_____

_____

_____

Chapter 3

Freedom from Blaming God

We prayed so hard for our son. I would cry out to God at work, in my car, at home. We continually laid hands on him and called on the elders of our church who anointed him with oil. We had friends pray for him, come to our home and have prayer meetings where they prayed over him and laid hands on him. We took him to pastors whom God had used in healing people. We even took him to California to an awesome church that had seen many healings from cancer. We truly believed that God was going to do a miracle here on this earth, that our son would be a testimony to God's healing power, and his story would become an encouragement to the church and the world.

I remember one specific time where I was praying and God gave me a picture (one of the first of many that I have had since that time). I saw myself holding my son in my arms. I saw Jesus come up to me and gently take him from me and carry him away. I wanted to believe it meant that Jesus was going to heal my son, then would bring him back to me whole. I would never allow myself to believe it meant anything else because I never wanted to believe anything else. Now, I believe He was letting me know that He was going to be taking him. And, as gently as He took my boy, that He would care for him eternally. That he would be whole again, but not on this earth.

As I mentioned in the previous chapter, I had many regrets. I regretted the fact that we didn't pursue certain things that in my mind might have changed the outcome of my son's journey with his disease. But, at some level, it wasn't about what I could have done differently. My main thought process was to blame God for what He didn't do. My one and only Savior whose Word promises hope and healing, did not deliver what we asked for, even when we spent so much time on our knees, and had thousands of people praying for my son at one time. We did everything in our power according to what Scripture teaches about healing, and we had faith that God would heal him and had healed him, only to have that horrible disease take him from us. When my son died, I felt like my Heavenly Father had let us down. He was supposed to have our backs, because of His great love for us. Even though we used every form of medicine available to us, I knew that at any time it was God who could and would bring healing. He was supposed to heal my son!! The "We live in a fallen world" statement fell on deaf ears. While that is completely true, in that time of trauma when we had trusted our Lord who has overcome the world, that was not what I wanted to hear.

After he had gone to Heaven, people would tell me that God had healed him, it just wasn't on earth. This would make me very angry. I would tell them that God knew good and well what kind of healing I was asking for, and this was not it! I would ask God why He didn't love me enough to heal my boy. I was so inwardly focused. When I look at Scripture now, I see that there are plenty of verses that focus on hardship and being tried by fire. I realized that those wouldn't be there if people didn't suffer hardships. Not all of those verses end up with people being healed, happy, and whole, going on their merry way. These verses say that the Lord will be with you, that He will walk through the fire with you, and that you won't be consumed by it. Most of us don't come out without being singed. It also says you will come out as gold, but gold doesn't happen without going through a big refining process, does it?

———— • ————

These trials will show that your faith is genuine. It is being tested as fire tests and purifies gold—though your faith is far more precious than mere gold. So when your faith remains strong through many trials, it will bring you much praise and glory and honor on the day when Jesus Christ is revealed to the whole world.

I Peter 1:7 (New Living Translation)

———— • ————

You most likely have seen others' children or family members healed while yours is taken. You've seen other people's lives restored while yours is devastated. You've seen others pick up the pieces while you lay broken. You have seen people's finances, marriages, homes, and lives restored while yours lay in ruins around you. You've heard people talk about their dark times when God came and spoke to them, but all you hear is silence. Have I experienced this very thing? Yes. Do I wonder why our family had to go through this? Yes. Do I still sit and ask God "Why?" even after all these years? Yes. Do I feel I've ever had an answer? No. But, I also understand that He loves those of us who are left on this earth enough that He will bind up our broken hearts and care for us until we are all together again. Indeed, Psalm 147:3 says, "He heals the brokenhearted and bandages their wounds" (New Living Translation).

I believe that God sees a picture we cannot see. My son sees this picture now, too. For me, I still am looking through a glass where I can't see clearly; but, some day, I will be face to face with my Lord, and I will know.

———————— ● ————————

Now we see things imperfectly, like puzzling reflections in a mirror, but then we will see everything with perfect clarity. All that I know now is partial and incomplete, but then I will know everything completely, just as God now knows me completely.

I Corinthians 13:12 (New Living Translation)
———————— ● ————————

I will always go through the struggles that come from losing my boy on this earth—missing him at our holiday tables, wondering about the wife he would have had, the grandbabies that I am missing out on kissing and loving. I will always miss his handsome face, his awesome speaking voice, his laugh, and his ability to change the climate of a room just by walking into it. He brought such joy to our life and the lives of others. At those times, when I am thinking about what could or should have been, is when I have to ask myself if I continue to trust God's word, even after I stood on those promises and it didn't seem like they were fulfilled. That's when I have to focus on pressing into the Lord, and am reassured once again and know in my heart that God's promises are true.

As my perspective has become less inwardly focused, and more heavenly focused, I have also come to realize that, just maybe, this wasn't about me. Maybe this was about how much God loved my son. As I started looking at Heaven as our complete reward, and not as a punishment, God began to open my eyes to how much He loved—loves—my son. He loved him so much that He took him away from the pains and hurts of this world. While I think of all the happy times that he has missed out on, I realize that those happy times on earth are just a small drop in a *very* large bucket. When I think of the beauty, joy, love, peace, and happiness—everything we can think of as the ultimate experience in our life on earth—if you multiply that by ten thousand, it still probably doesn't touch what God has for us in Heaven. This brings peace to my soul, and joy to my heart that not only is my boy enjoying this now, but someday our family will be together there enjoying it with him.

While much of this book is about my son, I also mentioned that I lost my parents in the same year, eight months apart to the day. My sweet momma struggled with dementia for the last seven to eight years of her life. She had served God with all she had. She was funny, creative, energetic, non-compromising in her faith, a loving and kind Pastor's wife—a faithful servant of God. Yet, she was left a shadow of the person who she used to be. My daddy was also a wonderful man. He was funny, loving, kind, and served God and people with everything he had. He had health struggles, too. Some were long term, but others came on late, especially the last two years of his life. There were times when I said, "God, these people I love, they have loved and served you most of their lives, and this is their end?!"

Blaming God seems like a good way to make sense of the unthinkable that has happened to those we love. The enemy of your soul wants you to believe that God doesn't love you, doesn't care, and has no plan for your life after your loss. The enemy wants to promote that sense of abandonment, to allow it to fester in our spirits so the wound can become deeper and deeper, the chasm of hurt and despair wider and wider, so our relationship with God becomes distant. He wants us to give up on all that we have given our lives to—the One we have given our lives to—and even go so far as to make us believe that God doesn't really even exist. Don't allow that fear and defiance to be built in you against the One who knew you before time began. Remember that God loves you, and He sees every tear you cry. Please, please, please, if you get nothing else from this book, I will say it again: Press In! Don't allow yourself to blame God.

Remember, while God's promises on this earth are true, they are also about eternity, and they are to prepare us for that wonderful day. Jesus overcame the world, not only so we can experience life abundantly on earth, but so that we can experience it eternally. Press In. Press *In!* God will give you strength. Not only to care for you in your grief, but to recognize when you are falling into a bottomless pit. The enemy comes disguised as a consoler, ready to help you feel more sorry for yourself, blame God, and make the chasm bigger. Time with the Lord will help you garner the strength you need to continue moving forward and not end up in a pit of despair that you can't get out of. God has a call on your life! Don't allow your desire to blame God steal that from you.

1. Do you feel you've blamed God in your grief?

2. When do you find yourself blaming God, and what are the triggers you've encountered?

3. What promises about eternity speak into your anger at God?

4. How can you shape your focus heavenward when you feel angry?

_____

_____

_____

_____

_____

_____

_____

_____

_____

_____

_____

_____

_____

Chapter 4

Freedom from Offense

At this time in history, we live in a
world that seems to take offense at everything.
Cancel Culture is widespread, and offense is
commonplace. It doesn't seem to matter what is
said or done; it will be offensive to someone. It
has become so easy to be offended, but even more
so when you are grieving, as our emotions tend
to be raw and lacking their normal buffers. In
my experience with grief, and in speaking with
others going through that process, I've found
that you will always encounter people who feel
they need to say that "one thing" that will make
everything okay; and, when they do, all of a
sudden their words will cause your life to be great
again. Perhaps there will also be a few who want
you to "snap out of it," feeling that if they use a
little "tough love," they will break through your
grief and your life will be normal again. Neither
of those things happen that easily, of course; and,
it is *so* easy to be offended by any phrase that rubs
your grieving heart the wrong way.

When I look back on those times now,
I realize that these friends were trying to be

helpful, and hoping that just maybe, they would be the one to say the one thing that would help me. Their hearts were in the right place, but the wrong words came out of their mouths. It's good to remember that those people love you and want to comfort you. It's also good to remember that sometimes it's alright to allow those words to go through one ear and come out the other, and not hold on to them, or allow them to bring offense into your heart.

It's also important to remember that unless someone has gone through the heartache you have, they will not understand no matter how hard they try. They may even be uncomfortable with your grief and this is their way of trying to make things normal again (for them, not necessarily for you). Sometimes there are those who have gone through some of the same heartache you have and will try to tell you what worked for them. Some of what they say may be helpful, and some may not be. Just as no two hearts are the same, no one's grieving journey will be the same. We all react to grief differently, and what was helpful for one, may not be helpful for another. I once told a friend who had experienced a loss that I had no words, but was praying for her. She shared with me that those were comforting words for her, because I wasn't trying to say something to solve her situation. Sometimes we just need people to sit in silence with us, or just listen and not talk. But, some may feel the need to share that "one thing," so do your best to be gracious to them.

While there are those people who want to come alongside and try to encourage us, there are also those who will stay away. When your heart and soul have gone through such a trauma as losing a loved one as I did, or a loss that has brought grief to you, we can find that people will have a tendency to walk on eggshells around us for fear of saying or doing something that will bring hurt or offense to our hearts. Sometimes this fear of offense can cause friends and family to be alienated from us for fear of saying the wrong thing. So, to avoid that possibility, they just avoid contact with you. It is important to be gracious to these people, too. Guarding your heart from offense while grieving will allow you to become easier and easier to be around again, though of course it is a process that takes time.

It is so easy to become offended at what is said, or even not said to us while going through loss. Still, you have to remember that while you are learning to live a new normal, most are trying to live a new normal around you, while continuing to live life as they always have. It can be an awkward time for everyone involved. It can also be a hard time just to be around life and people in general. I remember that when my son passed away, Thanksgiving and the Christmas season were right around the corner. I watched people laughing while they were shopping, enjoying the season, and I wanted to yell out, "Don't you know that my son has just died and my world has stopped? How dare you go on thinking it's alright to joyfully continue your life while mine has been devastated!" I had to learn that while my world stopped for a time, friends, family, and people in general were celebrating pregnancies, births, birthdays, weddings, etc.; and, just as we used to, they had a right to celebrate those things without having to worry that every time they said something, they had to stop and carefully check each word. Please know that I don't expect that anyone who's undergone loss to go out the next day and be part of someone's celebration. That certainly didn't happen to me! This kind of grace happens over time, as we allow God's comfort to be like a balm that, in each situation, brings gradual healing to our hearts.

Again, in my experience, this is part of the grieving process. Also, please know that I'm not saying that people shouldn't be sensitive to what has happened to you. There is a need for that, but people also need to be able to celebrate their joys and victories without feeling like they have to downplay their joy and excitement every time they see us, or we start holding control over every situation, and our friends and family will start alienating us from celebrations—"Oh, we thought it would be too hard on you, so we didn't invite you"—and from life in general. As you move through this process, please allow the Lord to guide you through this very hard and sensitive part of life, and to give you grace to love people, no matter what they say to you. It will keep your heart soft towards them, and not allow bitterness to take root. Also, when you are ready, I would encourage you to be part of people's celebrations. To move through this grieving process and not be stuck, we need to continue to experience life, celebrations, and victories of those we love. Let them know if their celebration brings tears to your eyes, that you will be okay. Once again, as you are going through this part of the process— Press In!! Ask the Lord to cover you as you walk through this time. When you start to experience victories and celebrate again (and you will), you will want those you love to be around you, celebrating with you.

The last thing I would ask you to remember is, at some point, you may have to walk through someone else's heartbreak with them. You have the tools to know what to say and do, and what not to say and do, to help them through their difficult time (remembering that not everything you say to them will work for them as it did for you). God will give you the grace to walk through this as you navigate grief; and, if necessary, will give you the grace to walk others through also. About eighteen months after my son passed away, for the following two years, I had a myriad of friends who lost their young adult children. While I was still going through my own grief, God gave my husband and I the strength to come alongside them and lift them up. There is something about binding another's wounds that helps in your own healing. We found strength we didn't know we had, and while this was never something I ever wanted to be able to relate to someone about, I was grateful that we could be an encouragement to someone else's heart at their time of need.

1. What is the phrase that most offends you since your loss, and why does it bother you?

2. What do you feel the offending party was really trying to say?

3. What has been or would be the most comforting words for you to hear in your situation?

4. Knowing what you know now, what would you say to come alongside a friend in their loss?

_____

_____

_____

_____

_____

_____

_____

_____

_____

_____

_____

_____

Chapter 5

Freedom from Fear of Trusting God

The enemy of your soul wants you to live in fear of ever trusting God again for your loved ones. It can make you live a lifestyle of "waiting for the other shoe to drop." The longer the enemy can keep you contained in that fear bubble, the longer he can keep you from completely giving your complete trust over to God.

This is something that has taken me a while to be victorious over, as I was a fearful child and that translated to being a fearful wife, mother, daughter, sister, etc. It has been my kryptonite, so to say. It was something I struggled with during my son's illness, and then when my son died, it got worse. When my younger daughter would not feel well or need see a doctor, I would flip out with panic and worry. I also had to know where everyone was all the time. Our older daughter lived on her own, and I made her text or call me every time she left our home to make sure she made it safely to her home. I had to have control of every minute. My daughter finally lovingly confronted me with the issue, and the light started coming on for me. I have gradually been able to let go of that fear. To be very honest, the enemy still uses it against me, and sometimes I will feel fear start to creep back in. He doesn't want me to trust God, and will whisper, "You can pray for their protection, but don't forget, God let you down before, so how can you trust Him for anything?" That doubt would sit in the back of my mind every time I prayed for protection or healing of a loved one.

This brought me to a crossroads where I finally realized that this fear was affecting my relationship with my Heavenly Father. I could either believe that God knows the best for every situation and decide that He is trustworthy, or I could decide to harbor fear and doubt and not allow myself to trust Him with anything again. I then realized that as long as the enemy can keep me a victim of those fears it would be very hard to ever trust God again. I had to acknowledge my fear and realize that this was a tool of the enemy holding me there. It is subtle and you can be entrenched in the thought processes and fears before you realize it.

When I say that I came to a crossroads, it wasn't just whether or not to trust Him to answer prayers for my life and that of my family, but this devastation in my life brought me to a crossroads of whether I would even continue to serve Him with my life. I have been a follower of Jesus nearly all my life. My Daddy was a pastor from the time I was born until the day he retired in his seventies, and I was raised in a home that trusted God for everything, without compromise. My husband

and I built our lives and that of our family on serving Jesus, no matter what. When we lost our son, I felt like the God that I had given my entire life to had turned His back on me, didn't really love me, didn't care, and everything I had known was a complete lie. I had believed with everything within me that He would heal my precious boy, and when He didn't, it sent me reeling. I couldn't worship, wouldn't listen to worship music, and felt prayer was useless . . . Life as I knew it was shattered, even my deepest-known truths.

My decision at this point would affect my entire life from that time forward. It took me a long while, but one distinct memory I have was when I read John 6:66-68, where Jesus asked His twelve disciples if they were going to leave Him. In verse sixty-eight, Peter said, "Lord, to whom would we go? You have the words that give eternal life" (New Living Translation). I came to the realization that there is no one and nothing else to which I would want to give my life. Jesus is my Savior, my Lord, my King, and I would not want to give myself to anyone or anything else. While I had made a decision to follow the Lord when I was young, this decision meant so much more, because it wasn't something I believed because that's how I was raised. It was a conscious decision in the midst of such heartache and grief to say "yes" to Jesus when I could have just as easily turned my back. When I say "Trust God," I don't say it flippantly. I have experienced heartache and devastation that brings you to a place where you have to decide whether you want to trust God with your heart, your salvation, anything or anyone ever again. I know it is easier said than done, but that is where the act of "pressing in" really counts. Even when you don't feel like it, spending that time in the presence of the Lord will give you the strength to move forward, be more conscious of the source of those thoughts of doubts and fear, and give you the power to be able to overcome through the power of the Holy Spirit. Do I understand His ways and His thoughts? No. Have I decided that regardless, I will trust Him anyway? Yes.

I am reminded of the story of the servant, Hagar in Genesis 21, when she and her son, Ishmael, were sent away by Abraham at the urging of his wife, Sarah. Scripture says that they wandered in the desert until they no longer had any water, and she knew the end was near for both of them. She laid her son down under a bush, then went away from him so she wouldn't have to watch him die. God heard the cries of her and her son, and sent an angel to minister to them. I have read this passage in several different versions of Scripture, but in *all* of them, I read that God opened her eyes to see a well of water. I haven't seen any versions that say God provided a well of water for them. I've wondered if Hagar was so grief-stricken in the fear that she was going to lose her son, and maybe even her own life, that she couldn't see the water that was there, and their lifeline all along? It took God opening her eyes to know that there was provision for them in their grief and their suffering. How many times have we wandered around aimlessly in grief and devastation, feeling like our life was over because of what we've been through? How many times have we not seen the lifegiving provision because grief had blinded our eyes to all that God had given us all along? I believe it's time to open our eyes and see what God already has provided for us so we can continue to live and move forward. There is a river of life for you when you feel like you can't go on any further, when you feel your life has no more meaning because of all you have been through. His name is Jesus. Your life has meaning and purpose, and He will provide all you need to open your eyes and see it.

1. Since your loss, what have you had a hard time trusting God with?

2. What has your loss made you fear?

3. How has this fear impacted your relationship with God?

4. What is a practice you can do daily to remind yourself to trust God with your fears?

_____

_____

_____

_____

_____

_____

_____

_____

_____

_____

_____

_____

_____

Chapter 6

Freedom from Anger
and Bitterness

Grief can be your friend in the short term. It can be a shelter and a bubble for all that is going on around you. But, allowing grief to encase you or encompass you for the long term can eventually suffocate you, take away your life, your hope, and your calling, replacing those things with anger and bitterness that take root in your spirit.

The traumatic experiences that I went through affected all my emotions. It threw me into a real tailspin, as I've seen it do to others who have been through loss. Anger can be a side effect of loss that can make us foul and mad at the world. This is something I've seen and been through. Looking back I realize that it is not an excuse to treat people badly, or to take our hurt out on others so they can feel just a little bit of what we have experienced. As I mentioned previously, it was pointed out to me at my place of employment that I was being short with people to the point that they were complaining to my manager about the way I handled their concerns. I didn't see it, and couldn't believe that it was true. When I look back now, I do see it, and realize that it was due to the loss that I experienced.

I believe that when your loss is new and fresh, while it's not an excuse to treat people badly, that this can be a side effect. As time goes on, however, the enemy of your soul can use this to keep you in bitterness and anger, so he can write your calling off the books. God understands that you have gone through a life-changing trauma, and at the beginning you may take your hurt and frustration out on Him. I truly believe that He understands. He is our creator and He understands our physical, emotional, and spiritual makeup. The world will try to validate this anger, as the enemy wants to distance you from your Heavenly Father in every way possible. But your Heavenly Father is always kind, compassionate, and slow to anger. He is our example, not the world. I believe His grace was sufficient for me and is sufficient for you as you walk through this valley. Your friends will understand this *for a time* and give you the grace to go through it.

Our relationships with the Lord, loved ones, and friends are the most important things in our lives. Anger can tear apart these relationships that are so precious to us. If we allow them to, these emotions can make us caustic to be around, and can alienate the very people we love and value so much. Again, I will say this—"Press In" and allow the Holy Spirit to work His healing in your heart. The Holy Spirit is a gentleman and will not force this on you, so you have to ask Him to do His work. In my experience, this is the time you will feel least like making this effort, but it's so important. Allow the Holy Spirit into your life to take control. He will be like a soothing oil flowing over you. He will bring healing to your heart, and your emotions. Those feelings of validation will start to subside, and the love you feel for your Heavenly Father and those that you love will start to overtake you. Your heart will go from being "stony" to "fleshy" again. Depending on where you are in your grieving process, this can be a turning point in allowing the Holy Spirit to start to bring healing to these deep wounds and heartache that you have experienced.

Have you heard the phrase, "You can become bitter or you can become better"? There is much truth to it. How does one become bitter? I believe it is through allowing the continual barrage of grief, hurt, and anger to assault our soul and our spirit. If you don't seek God for healing, you allow it to take root in your heart. If anger roots in your heart, you may justify your bitterness, and you may never see a need to be freed from those emotions. The root continues to grow and go deeper and deeper, until it has taken up residence in your heart and soul. Here, we can find ourselves in a caustic state where our words are nothing but venom to anyone we speak to. We can be miserable to be around. There is no joy, no peace, no contentment. Only harsh words that cut to the quick, and cause hurt to those around us. I believe I may have been on my way to that point, at one stage of my grief. So much in me was hurting; and, in my opinion, everyone else's problems or concerns were ridiculous, and were nothing compared to mine. Looking back,

I realize I was someone that not a lot of people enjoyed being around—unless they were very gracious. If people felt this at work, surely my dear husband had to feel it at home also. (I'm very thankful for this kind and patient man that the Lord blessed me with. I'm sure it took extra grace to live with me!) I'm so thankful that bitterness was not allowed to continue to take root, but that my conscience, led by the Holy Spirit, and friends that came alongside us, helped me realize what was happening.

Now, if bitterness has been allowed to take root in your life, how does one become better? First of all, by realizing what has happened in your heart is a tool of the enemy to sideline and distract you from the calling God has on your life, and by asking the Holy Spirit to remove it from you. In hearing from others who have been down this road, it is not a fast or easy process. It takes grace to humble yourself and realize that this is not what you've been called to do. But, be encouraged! It will happen and it is worth it!! Time spent in God's presence makes all the difference in the world. When that bitter root is no longer being fed by hurt, anger, and misery, but praise, worship, love, and joy are filling you, it can no longer survive in your heart. Pressing in will bring healing, wholeness, and life. God can and does make all things new when we ask Him for help. You don't have to live in bitterness anymore. You can be set free.

1. Do you feel you may have become bitter because of your loss?

2. Have you hurt those around you recently out of anger or bitterness?

3. What can you do to begin to heal the bitterness in your heart?

4. What Scripture can you hold to for a promise of freedom from your grief?

_____

_____

_____

_____

_____

_____

_____

_____

_____

_____

_____

_____

_____

Chapter 7

Freedom from Comparison

I think everyone has a tendency to live their lives in comparison. We compare what we have against what someone else has. We compare our success against someone else's success. As women, we compare our weight, fashion, looks, happiness, etc., against what we perceive is someone else's success in those areas. And, as Christians, we have skewed perceptions of what others have, how they look, what they do, and how God has had a hand in guiding their path compared to ours. So often we have equated that to the amount of love God has for us, as compared to how much He loves the people who have that "ideal" life—at least in our minds. Sometimes we think that someone just sat back and watched while God just did His thing with them and "poof!," they ended up having what they have today without any work, heartache, or pain. We always think the grass is greener on their side, and don't know the backstory, or even what they are going through that brought them to the place in life that we think is Utopia.

Now, look at that thought process when you have experienced the loss of a loved one against someone who hasn't had that experience, or has been in that situation, but saw God do miraculous healing through an instantaneous miracle, the medical community, etc. I know from experience that in that circumstance the wheels in my head start turning and the enemy starts whispering those comparisons in my head, and telling me that God must not love me like He loves that other person, or else why would He do this wonderful, miraculous thing for them and not for my boy? Then I would think, *I prayed just as hard, fought just as much, and loved my child as much or more than they did!* The thoughts also came when I would see someone who doesn't profess to be a follower of Jesus experience what seemed to be a great blessing, when I have served Him my whole life and have had to experience this pain. When I allowed those thoughts to permeate my mind, I felt I must have done something or not been spiritual enough that God didn't do for my child what He did for another's.

I was living in comparison—even more so in my devastation. I still struggle at times, wondering why God favored those people—either protecting them from going through what I went through, or giving them victory when I had to experience loss. When I give myself over to those thoughts even today, I still ask God, "Why my child?" Please know that never in my life would I ever want a parent to go through what we did, or any child to go through what my son did, but still, my question to God has been, "Why did my wonderful, amazing son even have to go through any of this, but that person who seemingly has no real relationship with you gets to have the joy of all their children here on earth?," or, "Why is that child being allowed to live their full life on earth, and my wonderful child was taken?" Also know that even in my grief I would never want something to happen to another child instead of mine; but, rather, I have always wondered why mine couldn't stay here, too. I find myself in that pit of comparison. It's hard to get out once you find yourself there.

These thoughts can cause us to lose trust in the Lord and in His plan for our lives. They can paralyze us emotionally, spiritually, and physically to keep us in the same place and never let us move ahead into God's calling and plan for us. It's so hard to trust God with anything after such devastation, especially when you are comparing what's happened in your life to what's happened in another's. It's hard to trust that He understands, that He loves us, that He cares as much about us as the person who still has their family intact. I know I sound like a broken record, but the only way to get out of that pit of comparison is to Press In!! As long as you distance yourself from God, you will be stuck in the pit of comparison and never be free to trust God and His plan again. You will continue to forget that God has a calling for you that is uniquely yours. Your life story is uniquely yours, no one else's, and God will use you and your story for His glory. He will work your story out for good. Press In!! God will give you the strength to trust Him. With the strength of the Lord, remove yourself from that comparison "pit." Trust Him for what you have gone through—not what anyone else has or hasn't experienced. He loves you and has a plan for you, but you must Press In.

In the time since losing my son I have realized everyone has a story. So many have walked through the fire to be where they are now, or are currently walking through dark times that we don't know about, but they don't allow it to be seen. What we see when we see someone or their smiling family on social media or when we watch them from afar has little to do with the depths of what someone is walking through. I saw a picture once of a shiny red apple in a mirror. The reflection was what everyone saw, but in the back where no one could see, the inside of the apple was rotten. We don't always know the battles that someone is going through emotionally, physically, or spiritually, but this picture is something that I try to remember. It helps me in those times that I want to compare what someone else has with what I have lost. It's usually not what I see or perceive. I encourage you to allow the Holy Spirit to bring a check to your spirit when you start to compare. Something that I've found helps me is to pray for the person you are comparing yourself with. Ask God to help them if they're struggling, and, while this takes much humility—ask Him to bless them abundantly. It's hard to compare yourself with them, when you were the one who asked God to bless them! Much of the time they are in need of it way more than you know. When I do that, it puts the focus on them and takes it off of me, which I've found to be a big help in moving forward in this process.

1. Who are you comparing your story to today?

2. What are some lies those comparisons have led you to believe?

3. How have these lies interfered with your relationship with God?

4. How can you pray for the person(s) to whom you are comparing yourself?

_____

_____

_____

_____

_____

_____

_____

_____

_____

_____

_____

_____

_____

_____

_____

Chapter 8

Freedom to Laugh Again

My son walked through sickness and disease in such a valiant way. He was going through so much hardship, and yet he kept his ability to make a joke and laugh at things. You would think I would be able to carry that forward and laugh, looking at things through his eyes. But, I couldn't; and, what's more, I didn't want to, because doing that would rack me with guilt. I shouldn't be laughing when he was no longer here and couldn't laugh. I didn't want anyone to think that I thought it was okay or even appropriate to laugh, or, in some cases, even smile. To this day, when asked how my day is going, I have had a hard time saying that I'm good. I feel that hole in my heart takes "good" down to "alright" or "fine." While I've come a long way in my grieving journey, this is still one of the things that I deal with. This is one of the latest things I'm working through in my journey. I imagine many people think I say "alright" because of my job or maybe I've had a rough day, but it is actually still because of the grief that I feel. It is, however, something that I can take to the Lord and lay at His feet. Isn't that wonderful?!

I am gradually getting to the point where I can say I'm good, but it has taken a long time. I can mean it, though, because I know my son is good. I am always reminded that he is living the best of the best. He isn't experiencing hardship, grief, sadness, worry, confusion, pain—any of the things that we are here. Those things that we consider the best of the best here on earth can't even begin to compare to what he is experiencing in Heaven. He is worshiping around the throne of God almighty, hearing sounds and seeing colors that I can't even fathom. His joy is beyond anything I can imagine or try to compare with any of the joy I saw him experience on earth. I know he is beyond excellent, so it's okay for me to say that I am good. My son had an awesome laugh, and when I think of it now, it makes me smile. I know that Heaven has got to be full of some of the most contagious laughter that you can ever imagine.

Continuing in this guilt or condemnation is a tool of the enemy, and it is to keep us in the same place, to keep us from moving forward in our calling. We can only be free from this condemnation through Jesus.

———— ● ————

So if the Son sets you free,
you are truly free.

John 8:36 (New Living Translation)

———— ● ————

We have to always remember and realize that the enemy's number one goal is to keep us down and in condemnation, feeling guilty whenever we feel hope or joy. But Jesus will free us from those thoughts that continue to keep us in bondage. When we are free, we can move ahead into what God has called us to do. As I say this to you, I also say it to myself.

While I realize that this is not something that you can do when you are in the midst of grief, when enough time has passed, remember the things that used to bring laughter and joy to your spirit. I want to encourage you to be free to express yourself with laughter, with a smile and with a greeting, to give someone else hope and encouragement. Being that hope and encouragement to someone else truly brings a contentment and a joy that is inexplicable. Whatever devastation you have gone through, I am a testimony to the fact that joy and laughter can be yours again. God will take you through the fire of grief, hopelessness, and helplessness, and will bring you to the other side. Remember, we don't come through the fire without smelling like smoke or being singed. And, while we never forget the smell of the fire or the experience, we know that God was there to bring us through. Proverbs 17:22 says, "A cheerful heart is good medicine, but a broken spirit saps a person's strength" (New Living Translation). When my heart is heavy, my strength—physical, mental & spiritual—is at a low point. When my heart is joyful and trusting in the Lord, my strength— physical, mental and spiritual—is lifted. Nehemiah 8:10 says, "The joy of the Lord is your strength" (New International Version). You have a Savior who has been there for you through the entire ordeal you have gone through and are still going through. If you will remember Him, all that He has done for you and will continue to do for you, He will be your joy.

1. When was the last time you felt free to laugh?

2. What is one thing that used to bring laughter and joy to your spirit?

3. What is a practice you can do daily to remind your heart that a cheerful spirit is good medicine?

4. What is a practice you can do daily to remind yourself to take joy in the Lord?

_____

_____

_____

_____

_____

_____

_____

_____

_____

_____

_____

_____

_____

Chapter 9

Freedom to Worship

As I mentioned before, it took me a long time to be able to worship again—or even listen to worship music—after the loss of our son. If you have had trouble worshiping since the devastation that happened in your life, I trust this chapter will minister to you. Worship is such an important part of connecting with the Lord in fellowship, and stepping into a deeper walk with God. Perhaps you are not yet at a point to tackle this topic in your walk with God, and that is okay. However, it is important to rebuild your avenue of worship in your relationship with God, so do not pass it over completely. If you are not ready yet, remember to come back to it.

Remember, when you have gone through the devastation of loss, you have been dealt a serious blow. Worship can feel false when your world is falling apart around you. It's easy to think, "How can I sing of joy when all I feel is pain and sorrow?" This stopped me from wanting to worship for a long time. In my experience in the church, it seems we have come to believe that worship is something we sing on Sundays. It is so easy to let that simple definition become the entirety of what we call worship. But, here's what Scripture says about worship:

———— ● ————

Beloved friends, what should be our proper response to God's marvelous mercies? I encourage you to surrender yourselves to God to be His sacred, living sacrifices. And live in holiness, experiencing all that delights His heart. For this becomes your genuine expression of worship.

Romans 12:1 (The Passion Translation)

———— ● ————

Even in our grief, our life can be an expression of worship to Him! That doesn't mean that you are supposed to "fake" your way through life and pretend like all is good, or just ignore your emotions or what's going on in your heart. Our lives can be an expression of worship, whether we are experiencing the greatest victories, or the worst grief and defeat. It's not about your ability to sing, it's about making your life, all of your life, a living sacrifice to God. I mentioned before that I came to a crossroads. When I came to that place, I had to decide whether to continue to make my life one of worship to God, or to turn my back and do my own thing (essentially, to walk in rebellion). When I say that I wanted to make my life one of worship, it doesn't mean that everything suddenly became happy and joyful. Very contrary to that. I was grieving and grieving hard. But deciding that my life would be worship to the Lord meant that I was giving my all back to Him and I would work my hardest not to dishonor Him. Was I angry and upset with Him? Yes, but there is a difference between obedience and rebellion. I chose to walk with Him no matter what emotions I was going through, and honor Him and what He did on the cross. Walking in rebellion would have meant going my own way, doing my own thing, and thus dishonoring what He did on the cross.

Years ago, while our kids were still in school, our family found ourselves looking for a new church. After much searching, He brought us to a church where we had to drive an hour each way on Sundays. Not ideal, but because of His directing, we did it for three years before actually moving to that city which we now call home. At this church, crowds of people (including us) would get to church and stand and wait in the entryway until a previous service let out. Did we want to get a good seat? Yes, but our goal was not to come and see what the pastor was going to speak on, or to fellowship with our friends—though we would benefit from all of those things. We were not coming to church to get our needs met, or because we needed God to do something for us. We were there because we couldn't wait to meet with Almighty God and worship Him corporately— to give Him our praise, love, affection, and adoration. We worshiped in song to God, about His power, might, and authority; and, we worshiped Him with our actions, honoring what He called us to do. We were so excited to do so we (and many others) got to church an hour early! He was calling us to Himself. Before we were privileged to find this church, it had been a long time since I had experienced God's presence in this way. Even though for a time I was not able to worship due to the hurt in my heart, the intimacy of worship that I had experienced before my loss once again became a longing in my heart. Once I tasted the goodness of the Lord in worshipping Him face to face again, I never wanted to go back to where we had been before. Deep was calling to deep, and I could do nothing less than answer that calling to enter His presence. Of course, it took me many steps and many years to be able to worship Him freely again. I encourage you to Press In—step into His presence, obey His Word, and worship Him with your life. One day you will again have the freedom to worship in any way He calls you.

If you are struggling with worshiping or spending time in the presence of the Lord, I encourage you to start with putting on some worship music, and just sit in His presence. The more you do it, the more you will come to know His love and compassion for your hurt and brokenness. He will meet you right where you are, and will start to bring healing to the places in your heart that you have been cautious in giving back to Him. Worship music can open the door for you to be free to Press In to Him. When you Press In, you will find Him, and your heart can be free to truly worship Him again.

———— • ————

When you call on me, when you come and pray to me, I'll listen. When you come looking for me, you'll find me. Yes, when you get serious about finding me and want it more than anything else, I'll make sure you won't be disappointed.

Jeremiah 29:12-14 (The Message)

———— • ————

When we are going through the grieving process, we are so weak and His strength is all we have to lean on. I can't tell you how grateful I am for Him meeting me where I needed to be met. He will meet you where you need to be met. And, as He meets you in His love, His kindness, and His healing of your heart, you can experience a deeper love for your Savior than you've ever had before. Remember, He is all-powerful, all-loving, all-kind—your All-in-All. Without Him, we can do nothing. He is Beauty, Peace, Joy, Love, Majesty, Almighty. He is powerful and awesome. You are His chosen one. You have been through devastation, but because of Jesus and His victory on the cross, you can overcome and make your life worship because of the blood of the Lamb and the word of your testimony. God will continue the process of healing your broken heart through your act of worship.

A quick word on the healing worship brings . . . When the Holy Spirit brings healing to your heart, that doesn't mean you forget your loved one or that the grieving process suddenly stops. Rather, because He loves you and loves time with you so much, He will help you continue to move forward in this "new normal" that you did not choose but is now yours. God has a plan for your life. Don't allow the enemy and the grip of grief to steal that from you. Worship Him. Even if you have to start small, spend concerted time with Him, then in daily life—whether in the closet, the shower, the car, making dinner, or in church—worship Him with your whole heart and allow your whole life to be worship to Him. It can be life changing, and bring you to a point where your intimacy with Almighty God, and knowing His heart and His love for you, will soften your heart and propel you forward as you go through this process.

God sometimes speaks to me in pictures, giving me clarity in what I'm praying for or when I'm seeking Him. For those of you who are struggling with worshiping God since your life was devastated, I hope the following will be an encouragement. When I was coming before Him in prayer and worship, wanting to draw closer to Him, He gave me a picture of me coming into the Throne Room. It was beautiful and expansive, with many stairs up to the throne, but I was the only one in there. I had an audience of only one— Jesus. He was sitting on His throne. I knelt and bowed with my face to the floor at the bottom of the stairs and worshiped Him. Instead of continuing to sit on His throne, He walked down the stairs and just sat on the bottom step next to me as I bowed before Him and worshipped Him. It was just Him and me. His very presence was all I needed, and I knew the great love He had for me and how He loved the time spent with just the two of us, as did I. He doesn't need our grand gestures, just our hearts. Just spending time with Him brings healing, hope, and life back to a life that is hurting and broken. My worship of Him has become more about what He did for me, and not what I need Him to do for me. It is about Him, and not about me. When I think about what my son is doing in Heaven, I know his worship around the throne is exuberant, reverent, and awe-filled at the beauty and the majesty of Almighty God. That's what I want my worship of Him to look like.

1. When was the last time you spent quality worship time with the Lord?

2. How has God met you where you are in worship or time with Him?

3. What worship song do you find soothes you since your loss?

4. How can you orient your worship to focus your spirit on what God has done for you, and not focus on what you feel He hasn't done for you?

_____

_____

_____

_____

_____

_____

_____

_____

_____

_____

_____

_____

Chapter 10

Freedom to Sing and Dance

For some of you this might be an interesting chapter. You might be thinking, "I could never sing or dance before any of this happened, so why would I be able to do it now?" This chapter has nothing to do with your musical or rhythmic abilities. However, it has everything to do with breaking free from the grip of grief and the paralyzing consequences that have happened in your body, your mind, and your spirit. There is healing through listening to praise and worship and actively worshiping God, as I mentioned in the chapter on Freedom to Worship. But I believe there is even deeper healing that can come through joining in and singing praise and worship to God in your own voice, and allowing yourself the freedom to dance before Him. When you are singing those words, they can get down deep into your spirit, bring the truth of God's word and His love for you, and make those truths more real. When you let go and dance in worship before God, it is a physical expression that can set you free from the grief that has held you in it's grip for so long. While this is not so much about dancing as it is being set free from that grip, I feel actual dancing can be a "side effect" of the freedom that you have come to experience when you have not allowed the grip of grief to take over. Take a look at these two Scriptures that describe singing and dancing in praise before God.

———— • ————

Then He broke through and transformed all my wailing into a whirling dance of ecstatic praise! He has torn the veil and lifted from me the sad heaviness of mourning. He wrapped me in the glory-garments of gladness.

Psalm 30:11 (The Passion Translation)

———— • ————

———— • ————

So go ahead, everyone and shout out your praises with joy! Break out of the box and let loose with the most joyous sound of praise! Sing your melody of praise to the Lord and make music like never before!

Psalm 98:4-5 (The Passion Translation)

———— • ————

I love this version of these Scriptures! It is so descriptive of the freedom and joy that come from being released from the hold that grief can have over us. What the Psalms describe here is the goal. But grief will try to keep you trapped in a place where you have no freedom to sing or dance as an expression of worship to God.

For me, the freedom to sing was a particularly difficult part of my grief. I not only

didn't sing, but I struggled to listen to praise
and worship music for quite a long time. Those
who know me well, know what big deal this was
for me. I have been singing for nearly as long
as I have been able to speak. I started singing
harmony by ear when I was only four years old. I
have been able to play the piano by note or by ear
since I was six years old. I have grown up singing
in church, going around the country singing with
my family, have been a worship leader, and have
played and sung on worship teams for many years.
Please know that I am not bragging, but am trying
to explain that singing and music is part of my
DNA and it would seem strange to completely
leave that out of my life.

But grief and unbelief caused me to
leave it behind for a time. When my son started
radiation, I prayed and asked God that He would
do a miracle and make it so my son had no side
effects from it. I believed with everything within
me that God would hear my prayer and that He
would honor it and answer it. A couple of hours
after his first treatment, my son went to work,
then called my husband and let him know that he
had just been sick. I remember my husband was
playing praise music, as we had decided that that
would be part of the culture of our home—to fill
it with songs of praise and worship and Scriptures
of healing. I went to the stereo and turned it
off. My husband asked why, and I said, "Because
none of it's true." That was my first of a long list
of experiences with feeling anger at God. I felt
if God wasn't going to answer my prayer, then I
would not listen to His music. If my husband was
playing something on the radio or other media

and I'd catch myself humming along, I would deliberately stop. I think at the time, it was my way of trying to control God, saying, "If You won't, then I won't . . ."

In this horrible time in my life, I got to the point that I just couldn't listen to songs that sounded like they were happy and pleased with what God had done for them. I know it was out of anger, frustration, and rebellion towards God, but also every song to me sounded "trite" and "fluffy." Granted, I had no idea what the story was behind the person who had written the song or what the impetus was to write it. I was entrenched in my grief and my story. I never thought of the possibility that the song I thought was trite, was written out of grief or hurt, due to the composer's story. Ironically, while I was still struggling with whether I even thought God loved me and was in the midst of my decision whether or not to continue to follow Him, the only songs I really wanted to be within earshot were songs of His power, His majesty, and His greatness. I needed to be reassured of the power of Almighty God, to know that He was fighting for my son, and that He was the Victor. As time passed, I started to be able to move forward in my own grieving process and was able to start listening to those songs again. Even though I thought some of it was still trite, I lost my intolerance of it that I had in the beginning. I started to sing along, then I started worshiping with my voice again. As I did, my heart started to become softened, and more and more receptive to the Holy Spirit, the still small voice that was calling for me to bring healing and walk in this "new normal" in the grace that God had provided.

Singing can be an outward expression of what God is doing in your spirit. I want to encourage you to sing out. It may not always be praise and worship, it may just be a song you like or it might be singing "kiddie" songs with your children. Whether you are a closet or a shower singer, or you are on a worship team, or do it professionally. Whether you sing a simple song, or sing an aria, whether you sing worship songs or sing your favorite song, just sing. It can bring joy to your heart and bring release from the grip of grief, just as the Psalms describe.

As for the freedom to dance in praise and worship, I didn't even know what it was until I experienced it at a church many years into my walk with the Lord. I remember my dad speaking of people dancing before the Lord, back in the "old days" when he was a young man. It always brought such joy to his face when he would tell those stories. When I was growing up, dancing before the Lord was something that was preached about that David did in Scripture, or something that happened in the great revivals, but was not something that was really practiced in our churches. When I got married, my husband and I were worship pastors for several years. We had the privilege of leading people into God's presence together; but still, dancing in church was not something that was practiced. We had always been in churches where dancing was more of a recreational activity, and not something you did in church or before God. After several years we transitioned from church ministry to being "regular church attendees." Long before losing our son, the Lord led us to a church where dancing before Him was not just accepted, it was a regular practice during our Worship Services. I still remember when I started dancing—it felt a little awkward at first, but as it became part of my worship before the Lord, there was a freedom in my spirit that I had never felt before. Even now, thinking about it brings a smile to my face. There was a freedom to love and worship God with my whole being, not just my voice and not just by raising my hands, but with everything I had. I felt total freedom. That was one of the most amazing seasons of my life, and I can't forget all that God did for me in that time.

After losing our son, I felt that there was no way ever that I would want to dance again—before the Lord, or for any other reason. The devastating grief we go through and the guilt that I spoke of before, have a way of holding us down. They have a way of taking away our ability to keep moving forward, to live, hope and enjoy the other amazing blessings in our lives, and . . . to dance. Experience the total freedom and liberation into what God's called you, and don't allow grief to hold you back from it. As I've mentioned many times, while processing grief and adjusting to the shock of a "new normal" takes time, I believe the only way we can be victorious is to continue moving forward, step by step, to freedom. Allow the Holy Spirit to continue to walk you through the process, so that grief does not hold you in one place forever.

So many times, I've seen the phrase "Dance like no one is watching." It took me a long time to get to that place, but I finally got to the place where I could dance again. I'm not a great dancer, but when my daughters got married, I danced at both of their receptions as much as I could, and had the best time. I actually prefer to be a closet dancer, though. If no one is around, that's the best time for me to come out of my shell. If I am playing a praise song I will dance before the Lord, or if a favorite song comes on, I will just dance for the fun of it. For me there is a freedom in dancing like no other. When you are at that place in your process, I encourage you to dance and experience the freedom and joy that comes with it. It can be awkward at first, but if it's just you and God, who really cares? However you are able to dance, then just dance. For me, this wasn't so much about the actual dance, but rather, it was symbolic of the freedom in knowing that I was not stagnant, but was continuing to move forward in this grieving process.

Remember, you were made to praise and worship Him. Singing and dancing as part of your worship is an outward expression of hope, freedom, joy, truth, and declaration—all things that are sitting inside you waiting to come out. This expression is your triumph over the part of grief that wants to enslave you; it stomps on the head of the enemy. So, I implore you, spend time with the Lord, pressing into Him in praise and in worship; and, in doing so, I believe you will find the freedom to sing and to dance before Him.

1. Do you find yourself shying away from singing or dancing since your loss?

2. Did you enjoy singing and dancing before your loss?

3. What song can you think of that is an expression of what God is doing in your spirit?

4. What step can you take away from the shackles of grief toward being free to dance?

_____

_____

_____

_____

_____

_____

_____

_____

_____

_____

_____

_____

_____

Chapter 11

Freedom to Live Again

"I'm sorry, there's nothing more we can do," Jon's doctor told us, one horrible day. I remember yelling out "No!," in the doctor's office when he gave our son that news. Up until that time, we had fought this horrendous disease for over two years and had used every form of medicine at our disposal (chemo, radiation, stem cell transplant, etc.), and believed that Jon was going to be whole—however God chose to do it. I remember that when my son got the news, and the doctor said there was nothing more they could do, he turned to the doctor and said "There's still God." Jon was not giving up, and neither would we. We had friends who helped pay for a trip to California to a church that has seen many healed of cancer. People there prayed over him and gave us hope. We also took him to a church in our city where the pastor had seen his son raised after he had passed away, and we were still believing that he would be healed. Yet just a few weeks after that, he was gone.

From the moment the doctor gave us the news, I lived in a fog of denial believing that

God was still going to make this right, and Jon would be a testimony to God's healing power. I wanted everything to be normal again. I wanted Jon to smile, laugh, make us laugh, be with his friends, and go serve God in how he had been called. I remember having to tell our girls, and how breaking the news to them brought grief to my heart, as it was so very hard for them to hear. Nothing made sense, and it all felt like it was nothing but a bad dream that I would awaken from at some point, and Jon would be fine, whole, and well, and would go around the world testifying about what God had done for him. Somewhere in between all of this, the church he was serving at and planning a missions training ministry with, licensed him as a pastor. He was so sick at the time he could hardly stand, but he did it. Again, we prayed over him, believing that this couldn't be all there was—God had plans for him. A couple of weeks before he passed away, Jon's friends invited him to a prayer meeting. We were so excited that he felt he could go. After he passed away, Jon's friends told us that he prayed over each of them that night. It really didn't surprise us, as that was just so "Jon" to do something like that. His heart was for those friends he had done so much life with.

I remember the last few days calling one of my friends and telling her that if God didn't do something, my boy was going to die. She encouraged me to call the doctor's office, who we were in continual communication with, at that point. They asked us to bring Jon in. We took our son to the hospital for what would be the last time. The doctors and nurses tried to let us know that this really was the end and that there was nothing more that could be done except to make our son comfortable. I remember getting so angry at them, telling them that God was going to do a miracle, and that they were wrong. I imagine every person who came out of his room said, "Be careful what you say to Mrs. Hutchison," because every person who came to his room to tell us how sorry they were, I would put them in their place, and tell them that we were not giving up hope. We actually never came home with him again, as He went into the presence of Jesus a couple of days later. God chose to take him while he was in the hospital. We called my son's best friends who had gone all over the world with him on missions trips, and had helped with taking him to chemo appointments, and let them know so they could tell him goodbye. We had friends and family who came to the hospital and surrounded us with love and prayer. I remember a group of us standing around Jon's bed and I thanked God for being so good. Did I really believe it at the time? No, but I was not going to allow the enemy to have any victory in this. God was still going to be glorified (obviously God's grace was heavy on us at that time, and my "anger phase" in my grieving process hadn't surfaced yet). The hospital was so wonderful in that they allowed us to be with him for as long as we wanted, and we spent much of the day there—going in and out of the room, spending time with him and allowing others to spend time with him also.

When it was finally time to leave, I remember crying and saying "But he's supposed to come home with us!," right before we left. When we got home, our best friends were waiting for us. We had posted Scripture all over our home on the walls. My friend asked if we would like it taken down before we got home. At first, we said "no," then changed our minds. At that point, those verses that had brought comfort now brought hurt and confusion. We were and still are so grateful for these dear friends who came alongside us, were there when we got home, and took care of so many things, I probably still don't know half of what they did. Amazingly enough, three weeks before Jon died, our neighborhood and yard was struck by lightning. It had taken out nearly everything that worked with electricity in our home. We hadn't had time or thought to get everything settled with insurance before Jon died, so our wonderful friends took all of it upon themselves and took care of it for us. Our church's Worship Department brought over everything we would need in the way of food, supplies, and a clean house to have out of town family and friends coming for Jon's service. We were surrounded by prayer, love, and caring friends from our church who truly made it so we didn't have to think.

While this is a bit of an aside, I want to stress the importance of having a church family. There is a reason Scripture says not to neglect meeting together with other believers. It's not just for the satisfaction of saying you went to church. I can't tell you the importance of connecting with other believers. If you are not in a fellowship of believers, find one where you have a connection. And, if you're struggling, then be the conduit. Being alone, and not having other believers come alongside and lifting you up when you are devastated is a very poor option, and makes it easy for grief to overtake you. You need the prayers, love, and support of those you have connected with, and you need to be the support when others need it.

When we returned home, I couldn't go into my son's room. Actually, it took me a long time to be able to go in there again. I just couldn't. It just hurt too badly. I was in no condition to go to work, physically or mentally.

For our son's service, we did everything we could think of to honor him and the wonderful young man he was. We also wanted to make sure that it ministered to people who knew Jesus, but also anyone who didn't or who was away from the Lord. Jon wore a penny "necklace"—a leather cord around his neck that had two pennies on it. When he would witness, he would give that person a penny and keep one. The one to them was to remind them that Jesus loved them, and the other one he kept to remind himself to pray for them. Jon's friends made single penny necklaces for every chair at Jon's service—there were around 1,200 people who came, so this was a monumental task for them. I still hear from people all these years later who still have their necklaces that they have kept. It helps this momma's heart to hear that. We were so amazed at the amount of people who came to honor him and our family. We actually invited the team of Jon's doctors to come to his service. We wanted them to hear the gospel and know what God meant in Jon's life. Two of his doctor's assistants actually came. When they came up to us after the service, I remember one of them saying "We had no idea." I believe they not only didn't know how many people would be in attendance, but also, what God meant to Jon and how his life had been used for the ministry of the gospel. I was just thinking about them the other day, and prayed that even all these years later, that God would bring Jon's service back to their memory and that if they hadn't yet, that they would give their lives to Him.

Even though I'm giving all these details, I was in very much a fog during much of this time. I really don't remember a lot, especially after Jon's service. Right after Jon's service, my husband, daughters, and I left town for a mini-getaway, where we could just be together. After a week, we took our younger daughter back to college—something that was really hard on this momma's heart, yet we wanted her to be able to do what she felt would be best for her, and this was what she wanted to do. Our older daughter had already graduated from college and had her own place, but we were so grateful that she was close to us, as those times she needed us, we needed her equally. Our girls loved their brother dearly, and this was so hard on them, but we wanted to be available for whatever they needed, whenever they needed us.

I don't know if we handled everything as we should have as parents, but then I think, who does? There is no play book for this, and if there was, I don't know that anyone would buy it. You do what you think is the best thing for everyone at the time with all the love and care in your heart, and you hope that you have done the best for them that you can, while you yourself are in the midst of the worst time of your life. We were not able to go to church for nearly a year, and if we tried, we would have to leave. Our son was so involved there, and every time we would go, we could imagine him worshipping in the front, or see his friends worshipping, which made it so hard. We just could not understand why he had to be taken.

A couple of months after we lost our son, friends sent us to Disney World for Christmas. We were so grateful to not be home at that time. I don't remember a lot of the trip, except that in the pictures we took I can see the pain in my eyes. We were having a nice time, but knowing the reason for our trip was heartbreaking. I turned fifty a couple of months later, and my girls and husband planned a surprise party for me. Our oldest daughter did much of the planning, as she is so gifted in that area, and even surprised me by getting our younger daughter from college and bringing her home. There were friends and family there, and while I so appreciated everyone's love and care to come celebrate my birthday, I barely remember one thing from that party, except my younger daughter walking in to surprise me. Fog surrounded me. Sometimes I think it is only by God's grace that I even functioned at all during that time, and probably for some years after.

You may wonder why I am sharing so much at this point in the book. When my son died, a part of my heart did also. I love my children so much, and this was almost more than I could bear. Please know that I am not discounting what Jesus did for me on the cross, or what God, His Word, and prayer are to my life, but this kind of grief leaves a hole that really cannot be filled in that way. As I mentioned before, that place at your table will always be vacant when you're together for holidays and special occasions. The joy of the day your loved one was born, and heartbreak of the day they left, doesn't just magically disappear from your memory because they are no longer here. It is a lifelong memory that leaves you figuring out how to cope. However, because of God's immeasurable grace that gives you strength and encouragement to get out of bed each morning and put one foot in front of the other, in time, you can learn to live again. He is the source of all you need to be able to do that. I don't know how people are able to live without the grace of God and go through such loss. Call on Him. I don't know how to explain it, as we seem to live in a world where we need the tangible in order to believe and explain things, but when I look back, I see and know how God's grace was so very evident in our lives.

Some of you, like me, have been caught in the tide of grief where you have questioned your faith, and some of you have allowed grief to overtake you in such a way that you have decided God no longer exists, and you want nothing having to do with Him or anyone who confesses Him as Lord. While I would never condemn you for the hurt your heart has been dealt, I would ask that you remember what situation brought you to this place of denying Him. It's not as if God existed in your life, then stopped existing because of your grief. God is real. He has existed from the beginning and did not stop when you went through your trauma. He has not left or forsaken you. The enemy's job is to get you to harden your heart and turn your back on Him, but God loves you! If you are in this place of denying God, I would encourage you to give God a chance again. He is with you, He has never left your side, and He will bring comfort and hope to your heart that has been so wounded. It's hard to surrender back something that you have held control of, but if you do, you won't be sorry.

Why can I talk about all of this now? Is my heart devastated in telling this story to you? Yes. It is so very hard to relive these things as I recall them; but, even in reliving them, I know there is a hope that cannot be shaken. There is hope because of Jesus. There is hope because I *know* that I will see our son again. I *know* that Jesus is real, and He will be returning for us who know Him and are waiting for Him. And I *know* that in the meantime, there is a call on your and my life that God has called us to fulfill. There is hope because you don't have to be shackled with the grip of grief. There is hope because there is still life in you. Whatever kind of grief you have experienced or are experiencing, with time, you can experience life again. It may not look like you intended, planned, or even dreamed.

This time and pain in your life may be taking you on a detour that leads you back to the road you were on before, but with a much different perspective than you had, to fulfill what God has called you to. You may find yourself on a completely new path that leads to you a completely different life, but a life that fulfills the call that God has for you. Either way, please don't give up. Please don't allow grief to win! I have found that you can still grieve, but grief doesn't have to be allowed to have control over you. You, through the power of the Holy Spirit, have control over it. If you are tired of not living life because of the horrible grief you have experienced, then perhaps the time is right for you to stand up and realize that it's a new day, a different day, a day that God has called you to rise up for what He has for you. Please know that I understand how hard this is. Getting up in grief day after day is overwhelming and exhausting, and it can steal away your life. For me, the most important part of this has been to recognize that fact, and know the schemes of the enemy to cheat you out of God's promise that He has for you. For me, the "whys" continue—even in writing this chapter and reliving memories about my son—but I've had to recognize that my trust is in the name of the Lord, and for me, "whys" will continue to come around. I also know that someday I will know as I am known.

The confidence of my calling enables me to overcome every difficulty without shame, for I have an intimate revelation of this God. And my faith in Him convinces me that He is more than able to keep all that I've placed in His hands safe and secure until the fullness of His appearing.

2 Timothy 1:12 (The Passion Translation)

Remember you're not in this alone, and it's important to allow the Holy Spirit to guide you, but to do that, please don't spend time in isolation. You have to spend time with Him. Press In!

1. What encouragement do you find in Scripture that is helping you overcome?

2. What promises do you find that give you confidence that you can trust God?

3. What do you feel God has called you to do or to be that has been sidelined by grief?

4. Does your calling have a different foundation with which to start from, since going through your grieving process?

_____

_____

_____

_____

_____

_____

_____

_____

_____

_____

_____

_____

_____

_____

Chapter 12

Freedom to See Heaven

If you haven't been able to tell this before now, this book is really for those whose hope and trust are in Jesus and for the hope of Heaven. Before I move ahead into this last chapter, there is something I need to share that I said I would come back to in Freedom from Regrets and Guilt. I know that there may be those of you who are believers whose loved one wasn't living for God when they passed away. I don't really know if my next statement will agree with many theologians out there, but I truly believe the Scripture that says it's not God's will that any perish, but that all come to repentance. Does that mean that I think God just takes everyone to Heaven and that there is no Hell? Not at all; but, I do believe that God gives opportunity for people in that last second before their final breath, to come to Him. I also understand that not everyone takes that opportunity, but I believe the Lord gives us that Scripture so that we can have that hope that our loved one is with Jesus.

I wanted to add this chapter at the end. It took me a long time to get to the point where I could ask the Lord to show me Heaven. I don't know why. Maybe for some of you, this was the first thing out of your mouth. At first, I just wanted to see my son again. I wanted him back, to be raised from the dead, and back in our family. Obviously, that wasn't part of God's plan. I've only seen my son well and whole in a dream one time, and it was shortly after he passed away. The rest of my dreams have been "waiting for the other shoe to drop" dreams. Those have left me feeling sad with a feeling of dread. Those are not the types of dreams I pray for, or ever want again, but the joy that I felt in that one dream is what I want to remember. In this dream, I was speaking on the phone with a friend who lost her child eighteen days after I lost mine. My daughters were there, and all of a sudden, they said "Mom, Jon is here!" I said to my friend "I have to go, Jon is here!" I could hear the confusion in her voice as I hung up the phone. My boy came into the room, and I was able to hug him and kiss his fuzzy cheek, and we sat down together. He never said anything, but I saw his beautiful smile before I woke up. I have had other dreadful dreams, but this joyful one is the one I will remember. I'm so thankful to the Lord for this one dream. I trust you have had or will have dreams that you can hold on to until you see your loved one again.

I have asked the Lord to give me a glimpse of Heaven. Maybe some of you have already experienced this, and have seen that beauty, joy, and utmost peace; but, others of you, like me, are still waiting for that time. Yet again, some of you are in a different place in your process and are not at that point yet. While I haven't had a dream or vision of Heaven, I believe the Lord has given me a glimpse in my mind as I have been in prayer, and has given me a different perspective of Heaven. While we do anything we can to hold on to this earth, as believers in Jesus this is not our destination or the place that we should cling to.

We also should not think of Heaven as the place our loved ones *had* to go because they were taken from this earth and that death is a punishment. As the Apostle Paul said, "For to me, living means living for Christ, and dying is even better" Philippians 1:21 (New Living Translation). I guess God gave me a bit of an epiphany and helped me realize that He loved my son enough to *let* him go to heaven early. It was at this point I realized that this journey was not all about me. It was about God's plan for my son, and His great love for him. While it was a horrible thing for our family and for me, my boy is experiencing the best that God has for all of us. He now sees Jesus face to face! We are not experiencing the best, but my son is.

On the twelfth of October, 2019, we hit year eleven of our new normal. As we do every year, we put a new arrangement of flowers at my son's grave. My husband and I made sure everything looked nice, and the flowers would bring color to a place that can be so sad and hopeless. As we always do, we held each other, and as we do every anniversary, and we wondered, "Why our child?" This year, we did not shed tears at his grave (that doesn't mean we didn't shed any tears). That was different than any other year. That doesn't mean that we have grown cold or calloused towards this day, but there is something that has changed for us. I put this on my social media page that year. I hope it will be encouraging to you:

———— • ————

This is going to be a lengthy post, but please bear with me. Many of you have walked this journey with us. You were there before the journey started with Jon. You knew him as friend, family, son, brother, classmate, leader, etc. You watched him go through horrible sickness. You, along with thousands of others, prayed for his healing and believed that it would be done. When God chose to take him home, you took care of us, prayed with us, loved on us, and gave encouragement on those days we couldn't even think and could barely breath. For you, we are so grateful!! Some things I've learned on this journey are:

1. Grieving never goes away, it's a lifelong process that you don't just get over.

2. Friends and family are so important in helping you.

3. God understands your hurt, confusion, and anger with Him.

4. And most importantly, God's Grace is there to carry you through all of it if you allow Him to.

This may be a radical statement, but I don't believe my boy is standing up in Heaven biding his time and watching over and out for his dad, me, his sisters, and their families. I do believe he has glimpses of us at times, but I don't believe he is sitting in Heaven playing his harp and making sure we are safe. I believe God, and the angels He has given charge over us do that. I believe Jon is in Heaven having the time of his life! He has the best of everything! He is hearing sounds and seeing colors we can't even fathom, his joy is uncontainable, and he is laughing with family and friends, *and* he gets to join with those family and friends and the Heavenly Host and worship around the throne of God Almighty!!

I don't know if the ten-year mark is the catalyst for me, but it seemed like after last year, this year has a made a way for hurt to be replaced with gratefulness; sorrow to be replaced with a lighter heart; and mourning replaced with a hope and confidence that God still has a call on my life that I can fulfill. I no longer feel like I'm asking God why He gave me this amazing child, only to break my heart and allow him to be taken, but now I can say "Thank you for the privilege to be this awesome child's mother, for his life and love and dedication to you, and that I know that I will see him again."

Does that mean I'm "over it" now? Never. Does it mean I've quit grieving? No. Does it mean I don't cry over him anymore? No. Will I still ask God "Why?" Yep. Will I still post an incessant amount of pictures leading up to and on this day? Of course! Not everyone who has gone through this has had or will have the same timeline. Grieving is like snowflakes—it looks different for everyone. This is where God has brought me. To our family and friends, who have walked these past eleven years with us and continue to do so—Thank you! You are more to us than you can imagine! And to my Heavenly Father—Thank you for bringing me to this place. I am so grateful that this earth is not the end, and for the assurance and hope for eternity. And, as always . . . Please say, "Hi," to my boy for me, and let him know how much I love him.

He has torn the veil and lifted me from the sad heaviness of mourning. He wrapped me in glory garments of gladness.

Psalm 30:11 (The Passion Translation)

Weeping may last through the night, but joy comes in the morning.

Psalm 30:5 (New Living Translation)

———————— ● ————————

I want to encourage you to live in this new normal—not merely exist. God has a call on your life that only you can fulfill. I believe I am finally fulfilling mine in writing these words to you. You can choose to continue to move forward in this process or you can allow the grip of grief to hold you in despair and stay there until Jesus calls you home. My prayer is that this book has encouraged you to start moving if you are held down, or to let you know that you are not alone on your journey, although yours is unique to you. I wrote a song a long time ago that I hope can be an encouragement to you. A part of it goes as follows:

Listen now, oh daughters,
let this be the day!
Cast off your old garments,
torn and old and gray!
Feelings of rejection,
put them all aside!
Put on garments white as snow,
you're called to be the Bride!

("The Bride Song" Copyright 2006)

As I finish this book, we are in a great time of turmoil in our country and in our world. We have been through a pandemic, and much grief, unrest, hopelessness, and insecurity in our nation. I believe we are living in what Scripture calls "The last days." While we are living in such turbulent times, I also believe that God is sending an awakening to our country and our world—the likes of which we have never seen before—before He returns to earth to gather up His Church. For me, while it is a concerning time, it is also a time of excited anticipation to see what God will do. I trust you are anticipating it also. I recently read from 2 Chronicles 5, where Scripture talks about the praise and worship of the singers and the instrumentalists. In their praise and worship, the

Glory of God came in like a thick cloud, so that the priests couldn't even continue with what they were doing because of the presence of Almighty God. My prayer is that you will continue to seek the face of God, and that in spite of, or possibly because of all you have been through, His presence will be so strong in your life, that you will have to stop, to seek His face, and desire to know Him as you have never known Him before.

While I don't know most of you who are reading this, I will be praying over you, that the God of peace will show you His plan, His purpose, and His love for you, and that you will be able to move forward knowing this, in the words of the Apostle Paul:

———— • ————

I pray with great faith for you, because I'm fully convinced that the One who began this glorious work in you will faithfully continue the process of maturing you and will put His finishing touches to it until the unveiling of our Lord Jesus Christ.

Philippians 1:6 (The Passion Translation)

———— • ————

I love you all. Thank you for allowing me to share my heart.

1. Do you have any insight God has given you on your calling in this world?

2. What verses about Heaven bring encouragement to your spirit?

3. Is there anyone in your community experiencing loss that you can come alongside?

4. Have you had a vision of heaven? Have you asked the Holy Spirit to speak into your vision? What has He spoken to you?

_____

_____

_____

_____

_____

_____

_____

_____

_____

_____

_____

_____

CPSIA information can be obtained
at www.ICGtesting.com
Printed in the USA
BVHW041346231121
622339BV00011B/479

9 780578 972572